John Christian

SYMBOLISTS AND DECADENTS

With 40 color plates

PARK SOUTH BOOKS
An imprint of
Publishers Marketing Enterprises Inc.
386 Park Avenue South
New York, New York 10016

Published by PARK SOUTH BOOKS
An imprint of Publishers Marketing Enterprises Inc.
386 Park Avenue South
New York, New York 10016

First published in the U.K. by
Thames and Hudson Ltd, London

© John Calmann and Cooper Ltd, 1977
This book was designed and produced by
John Calmann and Cooper Ltd, London

Reprinted 1985

Library of Congress Catalog Card Number: 84–61600

ISBN 0–917923–04–9

Printed in Hong Kong by Mandarin Offset Ltd

Introduction

THE TERM SYMBOLIST AND DECADENT ART is virtually impossible to define, so different in temperament, scope and achievement were the artists concerned. The only real common denominator was an approach to subject matter, a belief that a picture is neither simply an arrangement of lines and colours, nor a transcript from nature, but that behind a picture lies another order of meaning. To this basic principle all the artists in this book subscribed. Yet the same might be said of many earlier periods of European art: in what way were the Symbolists different?

It is worth stressing here that many Symbolist painters were acutely aware of their links with the past, and their work can often be seen in terms of this relation. Puvis, Watts and Böcklin, for instance, each wanted to bring new life to the classical tradition, while Moreau and Burne-Jones were deeply indebted to the work of the Italian Renaissance. But above all, Symbolism may be seen as the extension of the Romantic movement. Moreau and Redon relied heavily on Delacroix, and the Pre-Raphaelites, England's Symbolists, had many links with the English Romantic painters and poets.

At the same time, one of the most striking characteristics of Symbolist and Decadent art is its restless search for new modes of expression. The old subjects, if not exactly abandoned, were certainly seen in new ways, while altogether novel ones were everywhere introduced. Even the artists most deeply rooted in the past took enormous strides in this direction. Others went further, conquering fresh fields of imagination or, at worst, descending to exhibitionism, the most tedious aspect of the movement.

Although the origins of this search for new imagery lie outside the bounds of Symbolism, it was identified with the movement through its appeal to Symbolist writers and theoreticians, who in turn encouraged it immeasurably. This was particularly the case in France where the Symbolist aesthetic assumed its most cogent form, partly because Symbolism there was largely a literary phenomenon and partly because of the pressure of circumstances, political, social and aesthetic.

No text was so crucial for Symbolists as Baudelaire's *Fleurs du Mal*, published in 1857. It was important as a source of imagery, but still more as a definition of a state of mind, a portrayal, in the words of Verlaine, of 'modern man as he has become as the result of the refinements of excessive civilization . . . his senses sharpened and vibrant, his mind painfully subtle'. It was this being who, moulded by subsequent history, emerged some twenty or thirty years later as a Symbolist or Decadent. Political events were perhaps the most formative: the crushing defeat suffered by France in the Franco-Prussian War (1870–71), the horrors of the Commune (1871), and the overthrow of the old order by the Third Republic which followed. In more general philosophical terms, Symbolism was a protest against late nineteenth century scientific rationalism, and the materialism and smug moralism that flowed from it. As for the narrower sphere of aesthetics, here the reaction was against the limitations of Naturalism. J.-K. Huysmans, one of the most articulate prophets of the movement, began his career as a follower of Zola. Whistler and Fantin in the 1860s were already in revolt against Courbet, and by the 1880s it was recognized even by its own practitioners that an art of wider reference than Impressionism was needed.

The Symbolist standpoint is perfectly embodied in the movement's greatest poet, Stéphane Mallarmé. In the late 1860s Mallarmé had passed through an agonizing spiritual crisis from which he had emerged convinced that the only reality open to him was poetry. 'Poetry', he wrote, 'endows our stay on earth with authenticity and constitutes the only spiritual task'. It is therefore – and this was to be a crucial tenet of Symbolist philosophy – an activity which exists alongside, not in direct relation to the natural world. Moreover, since art obeys only its own rules, it need not, indeed should not, reflect external reality. 'To *name* an object', Mallarmé declared, 'is to suppress three-quarters of the enjoyment to be found in the poem . . . *suggestion*, that is the dream'. Hence his deliberate ambiguity, a quality which again is central to Symbolism in general. Symbolism can be, as it was for example, for Munch, a search for an image to embody a preconceived idea, but it is equally often an image to which we have to supply our own interpretation, and these images themselves often contain internal ambiguities, such as androgynous types or hybrids: Khnopff's *Medusa asleep* (*plate 29*) is the perfect example of this type of Symbolism in painting.

In September 1886 the term 'Symbolism' was given popular currency in a manifesto in *Le Figaro* by the minor poet Jean Moréas, but the movement's true manifesto was J.-K. Huysmans' celebrated novel *A Rebours*, published two years before. Huysmans' hero, Des Esseintes, was a man of aristocratic lineage and neurotic sensibility who, disgusted by modern life and 'American manners', sought refuge in solitude and every fantastic illusion that art and imagination could devise and money provide. Thus he came to be seen as the embodiment of 'Decadence', a word once described by Verlaine as 'all gleaming with crimson', suggesting 'the collapse into the flames of races exhausted by sensation at the invading sound of the enemy trumpets'. Des Esseintes himself was partly modelled on an exotic real-life character, Robert, Comte de Montesquiou-Fezensac, an aesthete and dandy in the Baudelairean tradition. Few could afford to emulate him in practice, but a generation identified with his fictional counterpart.

The artists whom Des Esseintes most admired, and whose works he collected, were Moreau and Redon, and it is with Moreau that any survey of Symbolist painting must start. Not only did he exercise an enormous influence but the sheer size, number and complexity of his pictures compels attention. He first made his name with a series of impressive works, heavily indebted to Delacroix, which he exhibited at the Salon in the mid-1860s. He then retired for a number of years, partly because of criticism of his pictures, partly in reaction to the devastating political events of 1870–71. When he reappeared at the Salon of 1876 it was to show the two Salome subjects which Huysmans described so ecstatically in *A Rebours* (*plate 1*). It is not difficult to see why Moreau thrilled the Decadents: the uncompromisingly cerebral, 'studio' nature of the pictures, their fantastic detail and mysterious tones, the over-civilized conception of intensely literary subjects – all this was guaranteed to appeal to the Des Esseintes mentality.

If Moreau was one of the fathers of French Symbolist painting, Puvis de Chavannes, only two years older and a fellow-student in Rome in the late 1850s, was the other. Like Moreau, Puvis was influenced by Delacroix and his follower Chassériau, and it was the example of Chassériau's frescoes in the Cour des Comptes in Paris that led him to devote so much time to mural painting, a field in which he carried out many official commissions. Even his easel pictures have the quality of murals: Huysmans described *The Poor Fisherman* (*plate 8*) as like 'an old fresco which has been eaten up by moonbeams and washed away by rain'. The demands of mural painting made

Puvis concentrate above all on pictorial clarity, and in a sense this precluded the subtlety which Symbolism demanded. But he is firmly linked to the movement both by his capacity for striking metaphor and his tendency to abstraction, to make his pictures, in his own words, 'not Nature, but parallel to Nature'. As we have seen, this was precisely Mallarmés ambition in poetry.

But it was Des Esseintes' other enthusiasm, Odilon Redon who, in the 1870s, evolved a pictorial language which seems the essence of Symbolism, at once subtler, more single-minded, and more convincing than anything seen before. Redon was an unsuccessful pupil of Gérôme with a strong imaginative bent that put him out of sympathy with the Impressionists, his exact contemporaries. He eventually found guidance from the strange visionary engraver, Rodolphe Bresdin (also admired by Des Esseintes), but the true nurse of his genius was the arid landscape of his family estate at Peyrelebade, in the Gironde, on which he was brought up and to which he returned regularly until it was sold in 1897. Redon was deeply read, drew constant inspiration from literary sources (the outstanding example is Flaubert's *Temptation of St. Anthony* for which he made three sets of lithographs), and was on intimate terms with Mallarmé and other Symbolist writers. But his art never lost its links with everyday things – landscape, marine life, flowers, even cheap illustrations, anything in fact that sparked off some train of allusive thought. It was this capacity to create magic out of humdrum reality that made him say he was a more genuinely ambitious artist than Moreau. Moreau could never do without the external trappings of drama and romance; his art, to quote Redon again, lacks 'instinctive sincerity'. Redon, so to speak, dives deeper and retains precisely this quality. For the first part of his career he worked almost exclusively in the black and white media of charcoal and lithography, but in about 1890 he turned, with brilliant results, to colour. All his pictures reproduced here date from this later period (*plates 4, 5, 6 and 7*).

For many, the greatest artist included in this book will be Gauguin. Beginning as an amateur follower of the Impressionists, Gauguin only became a full-time painter in 1883. At the same time, like so many artists in the 1880s, he began to seek an alternative to Impressionism capable of appealing to the heart as well as the eye. He found this eventually in the so-called 'Synthetist' style which he evolved with Émile Bernard at Pont-Aven in 1888 (*plate 11*). Gauguin brought a new dimension to the concept of Symbolism. For him it was not, as it was for Redon, a matter of dreams and allusions, nor, as for Puvis (whom he greatly admired), to do with giving concrete expression to abstract values. It was rather a search for a lost paradise, which he first identified with the primitive simplicity of Brittany, and later with the barbaric splendour and moral innocence of the South Seas.

At the end of the 1880s Gauguin was taken up by the Symbolists in Paris and acclaimed as the new star of the movement. His influence also spread among artists, notably the group who called themselves the Nabis (Hebrew for 'prophets'). These included Paul Sérusier, who had worked with Gauguin in Brittany, Maurice Denis (*plate 14*), Ker-Xavier Roussel, Félix Vallotton, Bonnard, Vuillard, and Maillol. They were artists of widely varying temperaments, and their contributions to Symbolism were mixed. The most significant figure in this context is Denis, an artist of great charm and elegance who reflects very strongly the influence of Catholicism.

In the 1890s French Symbolism entered its final phase and became an increasingly complex phenomenon. Le Sidaner (*plate 15*) is interesting as a painter who brought the Symbolist principle to bear on landscape; while the very sensitive Lévy-Dhurmer furnishes an example of Symbolist portraiture (*plate 16*). Another important group of painters were those who showed at the so-called Salon de la Rose + Croix, launched in 1892 as an alternative to the official Salon by that colourful and exotic figure, the 'Sâr' Péladan. Péladan was very much a product of his time: a passionate admirer of Italian art and Wagner's music, obsessed by Catholicism, fascinated by the occult, a flagrant exhibitionist and something of a charlatan. He had arrived in Paris in 1882 and made his name two years later with *Le Vice Suprême*, the first of a long series of novels. Soon afterwards he decided to revive the fifteenth century cult of Rosicrucianism and adopted the mysterious title of 'Sâr'. The Salons de la Rose + Croix were intended to give expression to his very decided views on art. According to the set of rules drawn up, the aim was to '*ruin realism*, reform Latin taste, and create a school of idealist art'. All the work shown had a strong Symbolist flavour.

Among the exhibitors were a number of Gauguin's followers and a group of artists, including Edgard Maxence, Armand Point, and Aman-Jean, who shared Péladan's admiration for the English Pre-Raphaelites and were influenced by their work. Péladan was also successful in attracting foreign artists, including the Swiss Ferdinand Hodler, the Dutchman Jan Toorop (*plate 34*), and a number of Belgians who had broken away from their own avant-garde group, known as Les XX. Of these the most interesting is Fernand Khnopff (*plates 28, 29 and 30*).

Khnopff and Toorop also show Pre-Raphaelite influence and it is not surprizing that Péladan tried to get the two most prominent English Symbolists, G. F. Watts and Edward Burne-Jones, to exhibit. Symbolism in England never had the clear-cut programme it did in France. It was the creation of individuals working in response to the prevailing spirit of the times, and the legacy of Pre-Raphaelitism which, like French Symbolism, had roots in the Romantic Movement. G. F. Watts was a Symbolist by virtue of his high-minded aim to paint 'ideas, not things' and his remarkable capacity for embodying these ideas in telling images. In some ways he is reminiscent of Puvis de Chavannes.

Among the Pre-Raphaelite group, the crucial figure was Dante Gabriel Rossetti. Although one of the original Brotherhood, he had never really been interested in their ideal of humble submission to nature. His was an interior world (he was of course a poet as well as a painter), and the logic of his approach was to lead him directly to Symbolism of a very specific kind. Others followed: in England, Simeon Solomon, for instance, was helped by Rossetti to realise a vision that was at once mystical and sensuous (*plate 25*). Whistler, the American painter who settled in Europe, might almost be cited as another case. Although he started his career as a realist and always went out of his way to deny that his work had any literary content, his very clear perception of moods often brought him into line with the Symbolists, especially during the 1860s when he was in touch with Rossetti's circle (*plate 26*). The artist, however, who emerged from Rossettian beginnings to make a really significant contribution to Symbolism was Burne-Jones (*plates 23 and 24*). Not only was he enormously prolific but for the first time he put English Symbolism in a European context by exhibiting abroad, particularly in Paris. He showed there fairly regularly from 1878 to 1896, corresponded with Puvis, received official honours, and was greatly admired.

Meanwhile in England an artist like Ricketts, himself a late product of Pre-Raphaelitism, could develop a passion for Gustave Moreau (*plate 27*). This influence is particularly strong in his illustrations, many of which were made for the poems of Oscar Wilde. Symbolism in fact was becoming truly international and by the turn of the century was a language spoken in places as far apart as Scotland, with its Glasgow School, Italy, pre-Revolutionary Russia, and America (*plate 38*).

Besides London and Paris, certain centres were pre-eminent. Belgium, for instance, made a vital contribution to Symbolism, drawing on the tradition of fantasy that runs through so much Netherlandish art. To contemporaries, especially if they belonged to avant-garde Decadent circles, the greatest Belgian Symbolist was undoubtedly Félicien Rops (*plate 33*), closely followed by Fernand Khnopff. Both embodied the international spirit. Rops was equally at home in Brussels and Paris and travelled widely. Khnopff had been a pupil of Moreau, knew Burne-Jones, illustrated Péladan's novels, and exhibited with 'Secessionist' groups in Munich and Vienna. Today both seem dated and minor figures beside James Ensor (*plates 31 and 32*), an artist misunderstood and bitterly criticized in his own time. In a sense Ensor is like Gauguin: a major artist who came to Symbolism from Impressionist beginnings and so adapted it to his own ends that he can never be considered purely in terms of the movement. Compared to Gauguin, however, he remains a baffling, and hence underestimated, figure.

Central Europe was the other major area of Symbolist activity, with Munich and Vienna as the points of focus. The picture here can only be sketched, but the main outlines tend to follow the pattern encountered elsewhere. The Swiss-born Arnold Böcklin (*plate 35*) played a similar rôle to that of Moreau (almost his exact contemporary) in France: a father-figure rooted in Romanticism yet seeking after a new subtlety of expression, deeply indebted to Italy (where Böcklin spent large parts of his life), and exercising a great influence on younger artists. His main following was in Munich, the artistic capital of Germany, where he lived in the early 1870s. Indeed his pupils Franz von Stuck and Max Klinger, exploiting elements latent in Böcklin, evolved a recognizably Munich form of Symbolism. Remarkable for its sense of menace and evil, this was to produce in the next generation the still weirder visions of Kubin (*plate 36*).

In Vienna the artist of overwhelming importance was Gustav Klimt (*plate 37*). Although quite different from the Munich group and considerably more important, like them and others we have noticed, he was very much a product of his time, not least in his preoccupation with sex as subject matter. Klimt reminds us also of two important aspects of Symbolism: its close links with the decorative arts and Art Nouveau, and its frequent identification with breakaway exhibiting groups. We have already noticed Péladan's venture and Les XX in Brussels; the Grosvenor Gallery, which showed Burne-Jones, Whistler, and Watts, offers an English parallel. The Munich 'Secession' was founded in 1893, and the Vienna version, with Klimt as president, in 1897.

In a sense, too, central Europe provides a figure to compare with Gauguin and Ensor: Edvard Munch (*plate 18*). Although Norwegian by birth and closely associated with Symbolist circles in Paris in the late 1880s and 1890s (he drew Mallarmé's portrait in 1896), Munch lived in Berlin from 1892 to 1895, and in retrospect his affinities are at least as strong with German Expressionism as with Symbolism. He is in fact a unique phenomenon, a Symbolist, even, in the choice of mental states he seeks to portray, as much a product of his time as Klimt; yet his mode of expression is so direct and free of self-consciousness that we tend instinctively to link him with the Modern Movement.

The connection between Symbolism and modern art was made in a different way by the last two painters represented in the illustrations who have not so far been mentioned, Picasso and Rouault (*plates 39 and 40*). They were among the many artists who became famous in the twentieth century, and whose early development included a Symbolist phase: other examples are Brancusi, Kandinski, and Kokoschka. Posterity has not been kind to the Symbolists, largely because the main tendency of modern art has seemed to be towards abstraction and against any form of literary allusion. The Surrealists are the chief exception, and it is significant that they admired the Symbolists. However, art-historians have recently begun to see in Symbolism an 'alternative tradition' to the classic sequence, Impressionism, Post-Impressionism, Cubism, Abstraction, and there is much to support this view. Not only did so many 'modern' artists have roots in Symbolism. Symbolism's rejection of naturalism and conception of art as a world *parallel* to the real one anticipated the basic principles of Abstraction.

It would be wrong, however, to see the Symbolists as simply marking some eccentric intermediate stage between Romanticism and the Modern Movement. They deserve to be considered on their own terms. They were men of ideas, and ultimately the success or failure of a Symbolist picture depends on the value of the idea it expresses. If some seem tedious or ridiculous today, this is hardly surprizing, for the Symbolists were setting themselves an almost impossible task, nothing less than the creation of a new pictorial vocabulary. The lesser men found the effort too much, and even the most consistently convincing (Redon, for example) could be silly at times. At their best, however, the Symbolists produced work of a new and haunting beauty; and whether they succeed or not, they perform a perennially valuable function, forcing us to ask ourselves questions about the nature of art itself.

GUSTAVE MOREAU (1826–1898)

1. *Salome Dancing before Herod (The Apparition)*

1876. Watercolour. 41 × 28½in (105 × 72cm)

This is one of two versions of the subject which Moreau exhibited at the Salon in 1876. They created a sensation and the composition has remained his most celebrated invention. Its swarming detail, jewelled colours, and atmosphere of lust and depravity seem to reveal his art at its most intense and characteristic. The pictures were probably inspired by the descriptive passages in Gustave Flaubert's *Salammbô* (1862). In turn they play a vital part in J.-K. Huysmans' famous novel *A Rebours* (1884). The book contains long accounts of both versions, which are among the most treasured possessions of the hero, Des Esseintes. The subject of *Salome*, a supreme example of the *femme fatale*, made an overwhelming appeal to the Symbolist imagination. It was also treated by Mallarmé, Oscar Wilde, Klimt (*plate 37*), and many others.

Paris, Musée du Louvre

GUSTAVE MOREAU (1826–1898)

2. *The Unicorns*

c.1885. Oil. 45¼ × 35½ in (115 × 90cm)

This beautiful painting seems to be imbued with a *fin-de-siècle* sterility, implied both by the subject, which refers to the mediaeval legend that unicorns were attracted by virgins, and by the very conscious use of sources: Pisanello, together with Cranach, clearly inspired the costumes, and Moreau may have been thinking especially of Pisanello's medal of Cecilia Gonzaga, which has the unicorn subject on the reverse. He was no doubt well aware too of the famous series of mediaeval tapestries, *La Dame à la Licorne*, in the Cluny Museum in Paris.

The picture is a good example of Moreau's passion for elaborate detail and his tendency to compose in terms of areas of abstract colour. The two interests were not always easy to reconcile, and many of his best pictures, like this one, remain unfinished.

Paris, Musée Gustave Moreau

GUSTAVE MOREAU (1826–1898)

3. *Sappho*

c.1884. Watercolour. 8 × 5¼in (20 × 13cm)

Moreau devoted a number of works to the story of the Greek poetess Sappho, possibly drawing inspiration from the revival of Gounod's opera *Sapho* in Paris in 1884. This illustration, provides a good example of Moreau's brilliant watercolour technique. It shows Sappho before she casts herself into the sea from the cliffs of the island of Lesbos, a despairing victim of love surrounded by symbols of poetry and death. The drawing once belonged to Oscar Wilde's friend John Gray, a minor poet of the 1890s who later became a Roman Catholic priest.

London, Victoria and Albert Museum

Gustave Moreau

ODILON REDON (1840–1916)

4. *Orpheus*

After 1903. Pastel. $27\frac{1}{2} \times 22\frac{1}{4}$ in (70 × 56·5 cm)

This is a late treatment by Redon of a subject which had been central to French Symbolism since Gustave Moreau exhibited his *Orphée* (Louvre) at the Salon of 1866. The critic Paul Leprieur described this picture as 'the image of the poet of every land and country, martyrized, misunderstood, but venerated after his death'. Both Moreau and Redon saw the severed head of Orpheus, continuing to sing after death, as a symbol of the immortality of art.

Cleveland, Museum of Art

ODILON REDON (1840–1916)

5. *Apparition*

c.1905. Oil. $25\frac{1}{2} \times 18\frac{3}{4}$in (64·5 × 47·5cm)

Flowers combined with the human figure were a
constantly recurring theme in Redon's work. The figures
here, which seem to have no specific meaning, are
curiously reminiscent of William Blake, a precursor of the
Symbolist movement in England. In fact 'A French Blake'
was the title of an article by Arthur Symons in *The Art
Review* of July 1890, which first introduced Redon to the
British public. Redon visited London in 1895, but the
British artist he particularly admired was Turner.

Princeton, University Art Museum

ODILON REDON (1840–1916)

6. *Buddha*

Before 1906. Pastel. 35½ × 28¾in (90 × 73cm)

Although Redon refused to espouse any one form of
religion, an artist as receptive as he was inevitably drew
on religious subject matter. A number of Christian themes
which occur in his work in the late 1890s reflect the
influence of Catholicism in Symbolist circles at the turn of
the century, and a group of pictures of the early 1900s are
devoted to Buddha. These may be linked to the widespread
interest in the writings of the German philosopher
Schopenhauer in France. Schopenhauer taught that the
only solution to the agonizing problems of life lay in
Nirvana, a pessimistic doctrine which appealed strongly to
the Symbolists and Decadents. Gustave Moreau, Gauguin
and many others felt his influence.

Paris, Musée du Louvre

ODILON REDON (1840–1916)

7. *Vase of Flowers*

After 1912. Pastel. $22\frac{1}{2} \times 13\frac{3}{4}$ in ($57 \times 35cm$)

With a few exceptions, such as a number of landscape studies, Redon worked only in black and white until about 1890. Thereafter, however, the exploration of the possibilities of colour became one of his main preoccupations. Flowers provided an ideal vehicle and he treated them again and again, notably in a long series of pastel drawings. In these his approach is objective compared to his earlier and more explicitly Symbolist work, but he still manages to imbue his subjects with a sense of mystery.

Paris, Musée du Louvre

PIERRE PUVIS DE CHAVANNES (1824–1898)

8. *The Poor Fisherman*

1881. Oil. 33½ × 62½ in (85·2 × 158·7cm)

This celebrated picture met with great hostility when it was exhibited at the Salon of 1881. Even Huysmans, the champion of Moreau and Redon, attacked it, although he admitted that 'despite the disgust which wells up in me when I stand in front of this painting, I cannot help being drawn to it when I am away from it'. It was, however, bought by the State in 1887, and in the 1890s came to be generally regarded as a masterpiece of pictorial symbolism. It was greatly admired by other artists, including Gauguin, Seurat, Signac, Maillol and his fellow Nabis.

Paris, Musée du Louvre

PIERRE PUVIS DE CHAVANNES (1824–1898)

9. *Hope*

c.1871. Oil. $27\frac{1}{2} \times 32\frac{1}{4}$ in (70 × 82cm)

Puvis' capacity to express an abstract idea in the form of a striking image is brilliantly demonstrated here. The picture is one of two versions, of which the other, showing the figure clothed, is in the Walters Art Gallery, Baltimore. The composition was inspired by the ending of the Franco-Prussian War, in which France had suffered a crushing defeat. Like *The Poor Fisherman* (*plate 8*), *Hope* was greatly admired by Gauguin, who kept a reproduction of it pinned up in his hut in Tahiti. The model for the figure, known in the Paris studios as 'Little Dobigny', also sat to Corot and Degas.

Paris, Musée du Louvre

HENRI FANTIN-LATOUR (1836–1904)

10. *Dawn and Night*

1894. Oil. 15$\frac{1}{2}$ × 10$\frac{5}{8}$ in (39·5 × 47·5cm)

Fantin's work falls into two parts, the naturalist flower-pieces and portraits, which reflect his training under Courbet, and a long series of imaginative figure compositions. Stylistically these look back to the Rococo, but they are important in the context of Symbolism since many were inspired by music, particularly Wagner's, which exercised an enormous influence on the Symbolist movement. Fantin also treated the subjects of Dawn and Night in separate compositions. A pastel of *Dawn* shown at the Salon of 1883 was greatly admired by the Symbolist writer and showman, Joséphin Péladan.

Birmingham, City Art Gallery

PAUL GAUGUIN (1848–1903)

11. *The Vision after the Sermon (Jacob and the Angel)*

1888. Oil. 28¾ × 36¼in (73 × 92cm)

This was Gauguin's first deliberately Symbolist picture and a turning point in his career. It is painted in the so-called 'Synthetist' style which he and Émile Bernard evolved as a more profound alternative to Impressionism when they were working at Pont-Aven in Brittany in 1888. Bernard in fact regarded Gauguin's picture as a mere pastiche of his own *Breton Women in a Green Field*, painted a few months before. But Gauguin went far beyond Bernard, using the new style not merely to paint a group of Breton women but a quality in them he admired, their simple faith. The picture had a great influence on the Nabis.

Edinburgh, National Gallery of Scotland

PAUL GAUGUIN (1848–1903)

12. *Contes Barbares*

1902. Oil. 38½ × 26in (98 × 66cm)

Gauguin's work after he settled in Tahiti in 1891 remained essentially Symbolist. The South Seas merely gave him a new vocabulary of forms and references. This haunting picture is a characteristic example, inviting us to find in it some deeper meaning, but tantalizingly refusing to make that meaning clear.

Essen, Folkwang Museum

ÉMILE BERNARD (1868–1941)

13. *Portrait of Madeleine Bernard*

1888. Oil. 24 × 19¾ in (61 × 50cm)

A man of many talents whose work passed through a bewildering number of styles, Bernard is best known for his association with Gauguin at Pont-Aven between 1888 and 1891 (see *plate 11*). His sister Madeleine came to Pont-Aven with her mother in 1888 and was painted by both artists. Gauguin also fell in love with her, to her parents' dismay since he was much older and married. She eventually married another artist from the Pont-Aven circle, Charles Laval, but died young in 1895.

Albi, Musée Toulouse-Lautrec

MAURICE DENIS (1870–1943)

14. *The Muses*

1893. Oil. 65 × 53in (168 × 135cm)

The strong overall design of this picture is typical of Denis,
and is found to a greater or lesser extent throughout the
work of the Nabis (Hebrew for 'prophets'), the group of
artists, amongst whom were Sérusier, Bonnard, Vuillard
and Maillol, who were inspired by Gauguin's 'Synthetist'
style, which was based on bold linear rhythms and areas of
flat colour (see *plate 11*). Denis' work, however, is always
sweeter and more elegant than Gauguin's, and often bears
a close relationship with Art Nouveau. The figures in *The
Muses* all have the features of Marthe Meurier whom Denis
married in June 1893.

Paris, Musée d'Art Moderne

HENRI LE SIDANER (1862–1939)

15. *The House with Green Shutters*

Oil. 23 × 31in (58·5 × 79cm)

Born in Mauritius of a Breton family that returned to
France in 1872, Le Sidaner entered the studio of the
academic painter Cabanel in 1880. Under the influence of
the Impressionists, however, he rejected his formal
training and moved to Étaples in Normandy where he
worked in isolation for five years, painting the
surrounding countryside. After making some figure
compositions on strictly Symbolist lines in the late 1890s,
he developed a Symbolist form of town- and landscape in
which he sought to convey the mystery inherent in
subjects such as empty towns and streets. From 1898 to
1900 he worked in Bruges, a town which fascinated many
Symbolist painters and writers (see *plate 16*).

Dundee, Museum and Art Gallery

LUCIEN LÉVY-DHURMER (1865–1953)

16. *Portrait of Georges Rodenbach*

1896. Pastel. 13¾ × 21¼in (35 × 54cm)

Although Lévy-Dhurmer began his career as a
lithographer and decorator (he was artistic director of a
decorative stoneware factory from 1887 to 1895), he was
an artist of great subtlety and sophistication, as this
portrait of the Belgian Symbolist poet Georges Rodenbach
shows. Rodenbach settled permanently in Paris in 1887,
but is seen here against a background of a canal scene in
Bruges, a city he treated in many of his poems and his
novel *Bruges-la-Morte* (1892), which was very famous at
the time. The portrait captures brilliantly the ideal of a
Symbolist poet, pale, haunted, and over-sensitive.

Paris, Musée d'Art Moderne

EDMOND FRANCOIS AMAN-JEAN (1860–1936)

17. *Woman in a Pink Dress*

1900–02. Pastel. 37¾ × 29in (96 × 74cm)

Aman-Jean trained at the Ecole des Beaux Arts where he
was a fellow pupil of Seurat. For a time they shared a
studio and Seurat drew his portrait which was shown at
the Salon in 1883. Aman-Jean's most characteristic works
are pictures of women seen as mysterious, pensive and
withdrawn, a vision which reflects his admiration for
Rossetti and Burne-Jones and his friendship with the
Symbolist poets. He knew Mallarmé as well as Péladan
and exhibited at the first two Salons de la Rose + Croix,
organized by Péladan in 1892 and 1893.

Paris, Collection M. Alain Lesieutre

EDVARD MUNCH (1863–1944)

18. *Jealousy*

1897. Oil. 26½ × 39¼in (67 × 100cm)

This is an example of Munch's ability to infuse a picture with some dominant emotion – fear, loneliness, melancholy, sexual awakening, or, in this case, jealousy. Particularly striking here is the use of red to convey the state of mind of the jealous man (a portrait of the poet, Stanislaw Przybyszewski), and the motive of the girl who flirts with his rival picking an apple, derived from the well-known imagery of *Genesis*. Although the treatment strikes us as more advanced than that of most Symbolist painters, the theme of the *femme fatale* is very typical of the 1890s.

Bergen, Billedgalleri

GEORGE FREDERICK WATTS (1817–1904)

19. *Hope*

1885. Oil. 56 × 44in (141 × 110cm)

Watts, a painter much admired in the England of his day, possessed in abundance that essential quality of a Symbolist painter, the ability to create a memorable image. The supreme example of this is *Hope*, represented by a female figure, blindfold but listening to a single string on a lyre. Once seen this famous picture is never forgotten, which helps to explain why it was regarded for so long as the epitome of all that was most regrettable in Victorian painting. It is interesting to compare it with the very different but equally haunting conception of the same subject by Puvis de Chavannes (*plate 9*), a painter whose seriousness and belief in the noble purpose of art had much in common with Watts's own approach.

London, Tate Galley

GEORGE FREDERICK WATTS (1817–1904)

20. *The Sower of the Systems*

1902. Oil. 26 × 21in (66 × 53cm)

Watts was always attracted by the astronomical and
cosmic and this picture, which dates from the last years of
his life, gives final expression to these ideas. It also shows
very clearly his strong tendency to pictorial abstraction.
The subject was suggested to him by the reflection of a
night-light on the ceiling. A number of Symbolists made
use of everyday images in this way, including Khnopff and
Redon.

Compton, Watts Gallery

DANTE GABRIEL ROSSETTI (1828–1882)

21. *Beata Beatrix*

1864. Oil. 34 × 26in (86 × 66cm)

This painting was begun before the death of Rossetti's wife
Elizabeth Siddal in February 1862, but completed
afterwards as a memorial to her. Rossetti described it as a
symbolic rendering of the death of Beatrice as recounted in
Dante's *Vita Nuova*, showing the event 'under the
resemblance of a trance, in which Beatrice seated at the
balcony overlooking the City is suddenly rapt from Earth
to Heaven'. Dante and Love are seen in the background,
while a bird, the messenger of death, drops a poppy
between Beatrice's hands. The shadow of the sundial
behind her falls on the hour of nine, the number which
had such significance in Dante's relationship with
Beatrice.

London, Tate Gallery

DANTE GABRIEL ROSSETTI (1828–1882)

22. *Astarte Syriaca*

1877. Oil. 72½ × 42in (183 × 107cm)

One of the most dramatic and successful of Rossetti's late paintings, *Astarte Syriaca* shows Venus, the goddess of love, not in her familiar Grecian form but as she was visualized in ancient Assyria and Babylon, fatal, cruel and mysterious. Her head is modelled from Jane Morris, the wife of William Morris, whose features appear in many of Rossetti's pictures of this date. His unhappy love for her was one of the causes of the depression which clouded his later life, and finds expression in the sombre mood of the present picture.

Manchester, City Art Gallery

EDWARD BURNE-JONES (1833–1898)

23. *The Mill*

1870–82. Oil. 35¾ × 77½in (91 × 197·5cm)

Few pictures demonstrate so well the parallel between the
work of Burne-Jones and European Symbolist painting.
Puvis , Gauguin, Denis, Le Sidaner, Khnopff, and many
others painted comparable figure-groups, although some
of these were in turn inspired by the Pre-Raphaelites. *The
Mill* is also Symbolist in its lack of specific subject. Its aim
is to evoke an atmosphere, one which many Symbolists
exploited, the nostalgia inherent in a summer's evening.
When exhibited at the Grosvenor Gallery in 1882 it was
accurately described by *The Times* as 'a work which . . .
reflects its truth only from certain mental states'.

London, Victoria and Albert Museum

EDWARD BURNE-JONES (1833–1898)

24. *Love Leading the Pilgrim*

1896–7. Oil. 62 × 120in (157 × 304cm)

Inspired by Chaucer's *Romaunt of the Rose*, this picture was designed in the early 1870s, begun in 1877, but not finished until twenty years later. It was Burne-Jones's last major painting to reach completion and was exhibited at the New Gallery in 1897, the year before he died. Like many of his late pictures, it seems to contain some private allusion, a comment perhaps on his progress through life as he neared his journey's end. It was not popular when exhibited and was still unsold at his death.

London, Tate Galley

SIMEON SOLOMON (1840–1905)

25. *Dawn*

1871. Gouache. 13½ × 19¼ in (34·5 × 49 cm)

The picture dates from the same year that Solomon published his allegorical prose poem *A Vision of Love Revealed in Sleep*. Two years later he was convicted of homosexual offences, a tragedy which wrecked his career and is already foreshadowed in the tone of the *Vision* and the epicene figure in the picture. The Symbolist movement owes much to Solomon's psychology. His androgynous type was taken up by Burne-Jones, who once described him as 'the greatest artist of us all', and through the medium of Burne-Jones's pictures passed into the vocabulary of European Symbolism.

Birmingham, City Art Gallery

JAMES ABBOT McNEILL WHISTLER (1834–1903)

26. *Symphony in White No. 1: The White Girl*

1862. Oil. 85 × 42½ in (214·5 × 108cm)

Whistler was by no means a conventional Symbolist, but, as J.-K. Huysmans recognized, many of his pictures convey a mood or atmosphere. *The White Girl*, a portrait of his mistress Joanna Heffernan, is particularly interesting since it was actually supplied with a meaning very much in keeping with later Symbolist thought. In 1863 it was shown at the Salon des Refusés in Paris, where it scored a triumph. Among those it impressed was the critic Castagnary who wrote that he wished to see it, not as a formal essay in shades of white, but 'something loftier, *The Bride's Tomorrow*, that troubling moment when the young woman questions herself and is astonished at no longer recognizing in herself the virginity of the night before'.

Washington, National Gallery of Art

CHARLES RICKETTS (1866–1931)

27. *The Death of Don Juan*

c.1911. Oil 45¾ × 37¾in (116 × 96cm)

The picture illustrates the closing scene of Mozart's *Don Giovanni* when the hero is confronted by the statue of the Commander and receives sentence of death. Ricketts wrote of it that 'the curtain . . . represents the rush of the wood instruments in the Overture'. He was passionately interested in music and had first seen the opera at the age of six. This is probably one of the earliest of a number of pictures which he based on the story. Although not Symbolist in the strictest sense, the picture's musical reference is highly characteristic of Symbolism, and Don Juan himself is conceived as a dissipated aesthete of the 1890s, bravely refusing to repent in the face of overwhelming fate. Ricketts' other source here was clearly Byron's *Don Juan*, and the picture reminds us of how much the notion of Decadence owed to the earlier Romantics, with their ideal of the dandy and their obsession with suffering and death.

London, Tate Gallery

FERNAND KHNOPFF (1858–1921)

28. *The Caress*

1896. Oil. 19¾ × 59¼ in (50 × 150cm)

The Caress, possibly Khnopff's most famous work, betrays his links with Moreau and the Pre-Raphaelites. The perversity of the subject is typical, and is underlined by the fact that the head of the sphinx is a likeness of the artist's sister. He was obsessed by her beauty and she appears in many of his pictures. Despite the thematic ambiguity, however, there is nothing accidental about the composition. Khnopff was a dandy and his pictures, like his clothes and his house in Brussels, were arranged with scrupulous attention to detail.

Brussels, Musées Royaux des Beaux-Arts

FERNAND KHNOPFF (1858–1921)

29. *Medusa asleep*

1896. Pastel. 28¼ × 11in (72 × 28cm)

As in *The Caress*, Khnopff here invents a hybrid creature,
part animal, part human, and gives its head the features of
his sister. Such hybrids, epitomizing the ambiguity which
the Symbolists admired so much, are found again and
again in their pictures. So too are images of silence and
inscrutability, although this example by Khnopff is
certainly one of the most compelling.

Neuilly-sur-Seine, Collection Félix Labisse

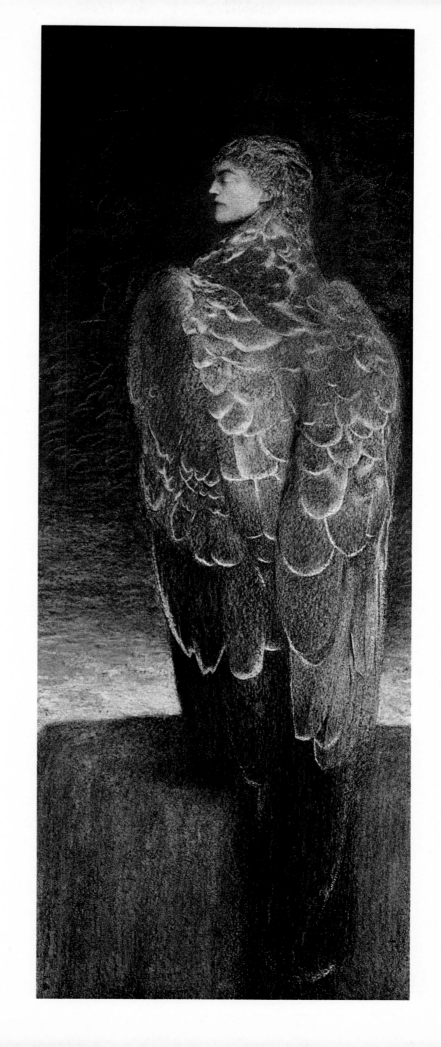

FERNAND KHNOPFF (1858–1921)

30. *Memories*

1889. Pastel. 50 × 68¾in (127 × 200cm)

The picture has the dream-like quality that memory
conveys and, as so often with Khnopff, evokes a sense of
tension and suspense. It was shown at the Hanover
Gallery in London in 1890 as *The Tennis Party*. Khnopff
himself was a frequent visitor to England in the 1890s and
admired English art which he helped to popularize in
Belgium. In particular he knew Burne-Jones, whose
painting *The Mill* (*plate 23*) has a number of points in
common with the present picture – the group of girls, the
evening light, the deliberately 'charged' atmosphere and
unspecified subject matter.

Brussels, Musée Royal des Beaux Arts

JAMES ENSOR (1860–1949)

31. *The Consoling Virgin*

1892. Oil. 19 × 15in (48 × 38cm)

Ensor fits uneasily into the context of late nineteenth century art: he is perhaps better seen in relation to the tradition of fantasy in Netherlandish painting, most strikingly represented by Bosch. He was certainly well aware of his links with the past, and in 1899 painted himself in the pose of a well-known self-portrait by his great predecessor Rubens. In the present picture he seems to be affirming his devotion to painting in a composition recalling the *Annunciation* or *St. Luke painting the Virgin*, both popular subjects in early Netherlandish art. The pale, pearly tones are typical of the palette which Ensort adopted in the later 1880s under the influence of the Impressionists.

Deurle, Collection I. Taevernier

JAMES ENSOR (1860–1949)

32. *Skeletons fighting for the Body of a Hanged Man*

1891. Oil. 23¼ × 29⅛ in (59 × 74cm)

Skeletons and masks constantly recur in Ensor's art as symbols of his sense of alienation, induced by the hostility of the critics and the public neglect which he suffered for many years. In this example, dating from his best period, the hanged man seems to represent the artist, cruelly treated by society which nonetheless argues about him in a totally futile manner.

Antwerp, Musée Royal des Beaux Arts

FÉLICIEN ROPS (1833–1898)

33. *Woman on a Rocking Horse*

1870. Etching with aquatint. $7\frac{1}{4} \times 5\frac{1}{2}$ in ($18\cdot5 \times 14cm$)

Like his fellow countryman Ensor, Rops inherited the Netherlandish love of the macabre. His special talent, however, was for the erotic (usually the perversely erotic) and the blasphemous. In these fields he enjoyed a great reputation. Baudelaire, Huysmans and the Goncourt brothers were among those who admired him, while Péladan, for whom he executed a number of frontispieces, classed him with Moreau and Puvis in the Symbolist hierarchy. He divided his time between Brussels and Paris, where he finally settled in 1874. His work may not be as profound as contemporaries thought, but it constitutes a valuable and often amusing reflection of the low-life of the time.

London, British Museum

JAN TOOROP (1858–1928)

34. *The Three Brides*

1893. Coloured drawing. $30\frac{3}{4} \times 38$in (78 × 98cm)

Toorop was born in Java of partly Javanese stock and although he left the East Indies at an early age there is an exoticism about his work which is quite un-European. *The Three Brides*, his masterpiece, shows an earthly bride between brides representing heaven and hell, a subject which looks forward to his conversion to Catholicism in 1905. The design is obsessively dominated by the rhythms of Art Nouveau, and the figures are like some grotesque parody of the Pre-Raphaelite style. Toorop came to England with the poet Verhaeren in 1884 and met William Morris.

Otterlo, Rijksmuseum Kröller-Müller

ARNOLD BÖCKLIN (1827–1901)

35. *The Island of the Dead*

1880. Oil. 43¾ × 61¼in (111 × 155cm)

The Island of the Dead, Böcklin's most celebrated picture,
was the final expression of a theme which had haunted
him for many years, that of a lonely villa by the sea. He
painted no less than five versions, of which another is in
the Metropolitan Museum, New York. It shows the artist
in his most strictly Symbolist vein, selecting and
recomposing elements from nature to evoke a particular
mood, in this case one of withdrawal and disassociation
from the world. For Böcklin in fact it was simply 'a picture
for dreaming over'. It was his dealer Fritz Gurlitt who gave
it the title by which it became well known.

Basle, Öffentliche Kunstsammlung

ALFRED KUBIN (1877–1959)

36. *The Turkey*

Pastel. $8\frac{1}{4} \times 5\frac{1}{2}in$ (21 × 14cm)

Kubin was born in Bohemia and after a turbulent and unhappy youth went to Munich to study art in 1898. The series of drawings he produced in the next few years, of which this is an example, show his disturbing and often macabre imagination at its most fertile and intense. A strong sense of the sinister was characteristic of Munich Symbolism, and Kubin was particularly impressed by the etchings of Max Klinger, whose nightmarish images owed something to his master Böcklin, but still more to Goya. Another influence was Redon, whom Kubin visited in 1905. Kubin later became a popular illustrator, but he never lost his weird imagination.

Vienna, Graphische Sammlung Albertina

GUSTAV KLIMT (1862–1918)

37. *Salome*

1909. Oil. 70 × 18in (178 × 46cm)

Klimt was the first President of the Vienna Secession, founded in 1897, and the dominant personality in the development of Symbolism in its Viennese form. His work reflects the Secession's concern with reform of the decorative arts within the prevailing style of Art Nouveau, placing extreme emphasis on surface pattern, the sophistication of which is underlined by their sexual content. In *Salome* he treats a theme central to Symbolist art in a spirit that owes much to Beardsley and the Pre-Raphaelites. Their work was shown at Secession exhibitions during Klimt's presidency.

Venice, Museo d'Arte Moderna

ELIHU VEDDER (1836–1923)

38. *The Lair of the Sea Serpent*

1864. Oil. 21 × 35¾in (53·5 × 91cm)

Vedder, who came of Dutch immigrant stock, left America
to study in Europe in 1856. *The Lair of the Sea Serpent* is
one of an interesting group of pictures with fantastic
themes which he painted on his return, when scratching a
living in New York. It is Symbolism conceived in
genuinely American terms (the monster might come from
the pages of Herman Melville), and is remarkably early in
date. Unfortunately Vedder did not develop this
imaginative field. Returning to Europe after the Civil War,
he settled in Rome and adopted a provincial Pre-
Raphaelite style. In the 1890s he executed mural
decorations in the Library of Congress in Washington.

Boston, Museum of Fine Arts

GEORGES ROUAULT (1871–1958)

39. *Le Repas*

1900. Pastel. $11\frac{1}{4} \times 11\frac{3}{8}$in (29 × 29cm)

Rouault, like Matisse, was a pupil of Gustave Moreau at the École des Beaux-Arts in the 1890s, and his early work is strongly influenced by his master. *Le Repas* (The Meal) in fact contains echoes of Moreau's Salome subjects (*plate 1*), although the picture seems to have no religious significance and also owes a debt to Dutch genre painting. For a few years after 1903 Rouault was curator of the Musée Gustave Moreau, and although his work developed independently, it always retained points of contact with Moreau, both in terms of content and style.

London, Tate Gallery

PABLO PICASSO (1881–1973)

40. *Life*

1903. Oil. 77½ × 50in (197 × 127cm)

Picasso's early work, the so-called 'Blue' and 'Rose' periods, has every right to be considered a late flowering of the Symbolist movement. In Barcelona in the 1890s he had studied reproductions of the work of Beardsley, Rossetti and Burne-Jones, and during his first years in Paris, although he was attracted by realists such as Toulouse-Lautrec, he also looked hard at Puvis, Redon, and Gauguin. *Life*, one of the most important paintings from the Blue Period, is a comment on the meaning of existence which finds close parallels in the work of Gauguin and Munch.

Cleveland, Museum of Art

JOHN CHRISTIAN AND BLACKER CALMANN COOPER LIMITED *would like to thank the galleries and owners who allowed works in their collections to be reproduced in this book. Plate 5 is reproduced by courtesey of The Art Museum, Princeton University, plate 26 by courtesy of the National Gallery of Art, Washington (Harris Whitmore Collection) and plate 20 is reproduced by courtesy of the Trustees of the Watts Gallery, Compton. They would also like to thank the following for providing transparencies: Cameraphoto, Venice (plate 37), Musées Nationaux, Paris (plates 1, 2, 6–9 and 14) and the Cooper-Bridgeman Library (plates 17 and 19). Plates 5–7, 13–17, 39 and 40 © by SPADEM Paris; plate 18 © by Oslo Kommunes Kunstsamlinger; plate 3 © by Galerie F. Welz.*